To:

Brenda

Love, Lauy

Know You are Loved.

Your Special!

Be Blessed!

Friends Always,

Lana Kuystermans

Nov. 10/07

Soft Petal Poems
With Heartfelt Love

Lana C. Kuystermans

authorHOUSE®

AuthorHouse™
1663 Liberty Drive, Suite 200
Bloomington, IN 47403
www.authorhouse.com
Phone: 1-800-839-8640

First published by AuthorHouse 9/20/2007

ISBN: 978-1-4343-3838-9 (sc)
ISBN: 978-1-4343-3840-2 (hc)

Printed in the United States of America
Bloomington, Indiana

This book is printed on acid-free paper.

This Book Is

Dedicated

In Loving Honour of the Late

Louise (Grandma) Flemmer

With

Many Special

Memories

Each moment you gave me

Was a Blessing Indeed

Lovingly

Lana

Table of Contents

Section One:

Family

Family

What is so wonderful as a family so dear
Maybe she's a sister or a brother so true
Loving and caring just for you

Yes, at times there are feuds to be had
But not usually long will you be sad
For mom and dear dad help us know
That love is the solution so problems won't grow

As we grow older side by side
Our love only deepens and grows inside
The bond that is made
Is to be cherished by all
For as we know
We reap what we sow
For family ties that are bound by love
Can only be lead from the light above

The love our parents show and teach
Is spread among us and does softly reach
By the long arm of life, a cycle does show
Back to mom and dad, love does go

Thank you mom and dad, brother and sister too.

I cherish you all, so dearly, I do!

Section Two:

The Important Ladies

In Your Life

Dearest Grandmother

Grandmother, Grandmother
Loving memories you do give
From the life you love to live
Strong and special in every way
Doing God's Work every day

Grandmother, Grandmother
The hearts you have touched
Will always mean so very much
Never forgetting your special embrace
Truly God is spreading His grace

Grandmother, Grandmother
You do smile so at ease
Knowing God is there to please
Smoothing the rough and jagged edge
Right to the end beside your bed
Prayer after prayer is said by you
And answer after answer does come through

Grandmother, Grandmother
Thank you for your words so wise
Passed on to us with heavenly ties
In our hearts you do live
Because of the love and hope you give

Grandmother, Grandmother
I would miss you so
With all your love, please don't ever go
God has blessed me especially through you
Making my faith continually true

Thank you Grandmother
For blessing our family and friends

Grandma's Love

Time is a treasure,

To hold in my heart.

I am so thankful you are a part

Of a life full of challenges

Whether far or near

You gave me strength

Year after year.

I know you're my grandma

I've loved you from birth.

Never letting me down

Your love is worth,

The sun, the stars

Everything to me.

Thank you Grandma.

God bless you eternally.

Sweetest Mom

Gentle and kind one person to me
Is my mother as strong, as strong can be
For she helped me through many trials of life
Loving and listening as I went through strife
She had her own problems, but never to fear
My wonderful mother was always near
Poor health and sorrow was dealt in her hand
Yet strong and content she did stand
Lovingly I see my caring mother dear
For courage and faith she did draw near
Never an angry word was said
Only quiet understanding was read
In my mother's actions and words alike
Thank you mom for you are my faiths delight
May you find comfort to know
Sincerely I love you so
May God bless you sweetly
Like you have blessed me
And may you be happy and well
On your life's long journey
I pray God shines on you
Till the end of time
Thanks again mom for being mine

Mother's Care

Deep within my soul,

I hold a special thread.

Of love deeply rooted,

From my mother, it is read.

As time hurried by,

A special strength grew.

My special Mother seeded.

The love that she knew.

Strong is her heart.

Strong is her care.

Now it's time for me to say,

Mother, thank you for being here.

I love you, mom.

With pleasure I pray.

That god pours his treasure on you,

Now and every single day!

Chosen Mother

Mom, I have a message.

With great care I have thought,

Of special moments throughout the years,

Because you did adopt.

A little child that needed love,

A guiding hand through my life.

From very young to this day now.

I hope you'll understand.

My love for you is very deep,

No matter where I am.

The memories made are sweet and true.

I am your biggest fan!

Thank you Mom for all you've done!

I pray it will never end.

Every moment far or near

I want it to be clear,

You've always been the special one,

And I'll always call you "My Mom"!

Caring Stepmom

A thank you is due,

For someone new,

Making this family whole.

At first unsure,

But ready to try,

My needing heart you stole.

First to my father,

Then to me,

Caring and sharing you sowed the seed,

Of trust, concern and tender love.

While holding my hand when in need.

As time unwinds you are a part,

Of God's grace looking down.

May love return and fill your heart,

As I'd like to crown,

A special note for all to hear,

Especially, I love you, Step – Mom.

My Mother-In-Laws Grace

I'd like to take a moment

To tell you how I feel.

Ever since I met your son,

Your blessings are real.

You are special and loving

Always sensitive and true

Thank you for your son,

He is the one for me too.

Thank you for nurturing

Our children with care.

As a true friend,

You are always there.

Deep within my heart

I hold a special spot

For a Mother-In-Law

I love you more than a lot.

Through your eyes I have seen

God's glimpse of eternal love.

I pray God holds your hand

As he watches from above.

Thank you, I love you.

My Daughter

It seems just like yesterday
You were only three.
Many pleasures we enjoyed,
While you sat on my knee.
You were sweet and innocent
My precious girl for all to see.
My daughter, my buddy, my kitten to me.
As you grew older, more lovely you got.
Whimsical, delicate and full of spunk.
You are my daughter, I whispered prayers
God is answering them daily in a special way.
Strong, yet content and full of love
Follow your heart, put God in charge
Know he will bless you as you march
Through life's open doors, for many there are
Anticipate love and adventure, carrying a torch.
You are my daughter,
I've loved you from birth.
Thank – you and God bless you from my heart.

Our Second Daughter

A star shone bright

Late one night

A second daughter born,

Was a mother's delight.

Your features were distinct,

Mother and father were linked.

To the sweetest little girl,

With the soft blonde curl.

God has a way,

With our second daughter,

Of projecting pure joy,

Being love and laughter.

Sweetheart, You are a blessing,

No one can deny.

I pray you are handed happiness,

Because you are the apple of our eye.

Dear Daughter

Honey, we love you,

And we're here to say,

Congratulations to you both,

On this very special day.

Your dad and I want you to know,

We've enjoyed you from birth.

You've given rays of sunshine,

And you are worth,

The sun, the stars,

That radiate love,

As you sparkle while teaching,

As god shines on you from above.

Your music, your sports,

Your talents for life.

Giving to others, love with spice.

Hold onto your dreams,

For dreams do come true.

May you be blessed,

For we care and love you.

You are your dad's dream,

And mine too,

Hugs and kisses,

From the bottom of our hearts!

Loving Mother

Quietly time passes,

As all mothers know.

A daughter is born,

And beautifully grows.

Once she was little,

But as time has its way.

Little she stays not,

For she's a woman today.

Now is her turn,

To give birth to a child.

Love in our family,

Is growing wild.

Love is sewn, as God does intend,

From mother to child,

With never an end.

God bless you, daughter,

I now am a Grandma, mother and friend.

Love you always!

Precious Daughter-In-Law

As time unfolds,

More blessings are ours,

Our son once single,

Has now shone like the stars.

Into our lives a woman with charm.

Has made my son whole,

As she rests on his arm,

A daughter-in-law,

So special and true,

Has made us complete.

For like her are few.

We care for you, We love you.

Your love is sewn into our lives.

May the thread of happiness

Grow deep and wide in size.

May God continue to smile,

Down upon you two.

For by the grace of God,

We have been blessed by you.

May God bless you always!

Love Mom and Dad.

Precious Granddaughter

Sweet little baby,

Soft and tender.

Smile a smile,

Will you remember,

The love that I give you

Now while you are small,

Gently cooing, yet growing tall.

Sleep precious baby,

Still and quiet you lay.

Quiet as an angel,

Watches over you today.

I love you, I love you.

In your sweetness you sleep.

I pray, God will keep you

Safe and complete.

As time you go through,

I surely have found.

Blessings are true,

And especially a blessing are you!

Special Granddaughter

Sweet little girl,

Precious child to us.

A wonderful gift,

From your parents, you see.

Breath of love at first sight,

As we did behold.

A beautiful Granddaughter,

Is here to hold.

Cute button nose features,

Sweet soft eyes too.

Granddaughter, Granddaughter,

You bless us, you do.

All through your childhood

And into your teens.

We've watched you joyfully,

And tenderly seen.

A beautiful person,

Inside and out,

Thank-you Granddaughter,

God bless you from our hearts.

Loving Great Granddaughter

Through time and measure

Our family has grown

Once just Papa and I

Precious seeds were sown.

For through the years

Our family roots went deep.

Nutritious rich soil as we did reap.

Bonds of love through family and kin

And now the branch that brought you in

A Great Granddaughter at her best

Is loved and cherished above all the rest.

In our hearts we carry your love

Your precious smile must be sent from above.

We thank you maker.

As we have found

For your gift of presence

As love does abound.

God Bless you, Great Granddaughter.

You're in our prayers.

My Sister

When times were good

When times were bad

A sister I knew I always had.

You'd pull my hair

Or perhaps cut it too.

And yes, you sometimes made me stew.

Mom calls us a pair,

Two peas in a pod

Laughing and playing – non – stop.

Close we grew, Our hearts only knew.

The closeness that precious time does do.

Secrets were told, I remember a few

You are my buddy; you'd take the cue.

You'd help me out, whenever you could.

Now I realize I really should

Let you know a heartfelt thanks

That you deserve above all ranks

I love you sister, I always have.

May God bless your tomorrows

In a splendid full way.

Thank – you sis and all the best

Sisters' Gifts

A special gift to me,

Is many a sister, you see.

For in the midst of sister siblings,

Is love, concern and honesty.

Few friendships are made,

As strong as ours.

For precious sisters,

Shine bright as the stars.

Our bonding grows

Through childhood years.

Now as women we reach

Afar with joyful tears.

Thank you sisters,

Each one of you

I love you all,

Completely, deeply,

And for the rest of my years.

May God pour His Blessings,

Through Heavens open windows,

Into your lives for all Eternity.

Sister's Bond

A sister's bond is what we have.

We share our family tree.

You now live far around the world

And yet you're close to me.

As fate unfolds,

Our love remains,

And joy grows stronger too.

I hope and pray the very best

Is coming to the two of you

As your wedding music plays,

My tears will overflow.

Bringing life and love today,

I can see your radiant glow.

Follow your heart, adventure at hand.

Remember sis, I think you're grand.

God bless and take care.

My love to you I send,

Congrats overflowing!

Special Sister & Brother In-Law

From the bottom of my heart

A thank – you is due.

I remember our visit,

With love it is true.

Sister and husband

I treasure the thought

From bingo to knitting,

Or just a long walk.

Time spent with you

Has rekindled my soul

Being in your presence

Has made me whole.

The laughter we shared

Is precious to me

I hope you are given

Life abundantly.

May God shine in your life,

And blessings unfold.

A special thanks again,

Sis and Brother in-law.

My Sister-In-Law

Into your family I came with love,

First to your brother,

Then all of the above.

Your Mother and Father,

Brothers and you.

My long time dream has now come true.

A Sister-In-Law, so special and kind.

A hug is in order, many a time.

I know when we met,

You had a sincere glow,

You make me feel good,

And I want you to know.

Your friendship of love,

Is held in my heart,

And I don't know where to start.

I guess I will say,

I wish for you,

The best of God's love,

Everyday through and through.

Thank you special Sister,

May God bring your dreams true.

Loving Aunt

Long overdue are my words of thanks,

For a lady so dear,

Whom in my heart, is always near.

From newborn up, she does care,

Giving her love year after year.

As the family grows, the signs do show,

My wonderful Aunt is quick to sow,

The special love that only Aunts can give,

Precious memories sewn through time that lives,

In our hearts eternal, God does share.

Thank-you Auntie for being there,

You in my life, whether far or near,

Shows memories of love etched with care.

I pray you are blessed gently from above,

Good health and wealth and dreams of love.

Special you are, and love you are too.

Thank-you Auntie for being you!

My Nieces Love

Sweet innocent girl,

A long, long time ago,

Came into my life,

As love began to grow.

I know you are my niece,

But heart strings say your mine.

I want you to know,

I think of you all the time.

As years did unfold,

My bond with you grew.

I can't think of anyone,

As special as you.

From childhood to a woman,

The joy you give remains

Deep with in my heart,

As life to my soul obtains.

A bond of friendship, love and care,

Thank you Niece for letting me share,

Your life, your dreams,

At times your sorrow too.

God bless you child,

I'll always love you!

Precious Little Girl

Deep in my heart,

Is the makings of love.

That spreads to your family,

I know is from above.

First your mom and dear Dad,

Were friends at the start.

A hug, then a kiss and then a tender smile.

Now your birthday has come,

I'd like to share awhile.

The completeness, the joy, the excitement too.

I'll always try to be there for you.

No matter where time does lead,

I hope you watch and grow

Into a beautiful woman

With love abounding I know.

God bless you child,

Mom and Dad too.

Thanks for letting me be

Auntie to you.

Section Three:

Cousins Connection

My Cousin

Early in my childhood

Which doesn't seem that long ago.

I learned I had a cousin,

The same age as me or so.

We often sat and played,

Or to the park we'd go.

Our mothers were the best of friends,

Actually they were sisters,

Now I know.

As we grew up in time,

Our paths grew apart,

But our love for one another,

Kept strong from the start.

In times of need,

I'd hear your words and say,

Thank you Cous for all your care

From that very first day.

Love ya always.

Special Cousins

We're very happy to say,

A special cousin is here today.

A new born baby,

To hold in our arms,

To smother with kisses,

Now a bundle of charm.

With eagerness hoped,

We yearned for this child.

The love in this family,

Is growing wild.

Our cousin and us have been blessed

It is true.

I pray this new baby,

Is blessed through and through.

May God shine on this child,

With understanding and love,

Because cous, I believe this child,

Has been sent from above.

Love you cousin and baby.

Good health and happiness to both of you!

Section Four:

Special Babies In Your Life

Sweet Baby Girl

Congratulations!

Look who is new!

A sweet baby girl

For mom, dad and family too!

A pure bundle of joy

All dressed in pink

Ruffles and bows right down to her feet.

With button nose features

And soft curly hair

To hold in our arms

She is so cute and fair.

Barrettes, bows and smiles,

Brings hugs and kisses too

We really are happy,

For all of you!

Congratulations again!

Sweet Baby

Sweet little baby,

Soft and tender

Smile a smile,

Will you remember,

The love that I give you?

Now while you are small,

Gently cooing, yet growing tall.

Sleep precious baby,

Still and quiet you lay.

Quiet as an angel,

Watches over you today.

I love you, I love you.

In your sweetness you sleep.

I pray, God will keep you

Safe and complete.

As time you go through

I surely have found

Blessings are true,

And especially a blessing are you!

Unforgotten Baby

My precious little child

A long, long time ago.

Left a void in my heart,

And a hole in my soul.

At the time I had no choice,

To another family I gave

A true treasure to hold,

And for me a heartache.

Never the less,

Time did pass by,

Never a night passed,

That I didn't cry.

I've yearned for this moment

Year in and year out

I could only pray

For the chance to say,

I love you, I love you

Sweet child of mine.

I pray God shines on you,

Till the end of time!

My Only Child

Many months early,

My baby came to me.

A pound or two at birth,

Years later sitting on my knee.

Life by a thread,

Holding on at birth.

The greatest gift given,

For you are worth.

The sun, the stars,

Everything in between

Words can't tell,

How important you are to me.

Shine, stand tall,

Grow strong and be sure

The love you give,

Will always return.

I will love you forever,

Only child of mine,

God bless you honey,

To the end of time.

Lost But Not Forgotten

Look in my heart,

Look in my soul,

See the love,

That makes me whole.

A child I carried

Many months later,

A child I lost,

Is sweet I remember.

You died so young,

You died so frail.

In my arms,

You were so pale.

You are in my heart

You are on my mind

Now angel's sing,

As you are a part.

Of heaven's treasures.

God's Eternal Love

I know he will keep you,

Happy, Content,

In the Heaven's above.

Section Five:

Important Men In Your Life

My Father

Looking into my life I see,

A father, special and kind.

When I was young I sat on his knee,

And stories he often told to me.

He was strong, yet gentle,

And very hard working.

And sometimes,

Off to the lake we would go lurking.

Boating and fishing, exploring too.

Love him so much, I certainly do.

He cares for me,

Like only he can.

Thank you dear Dad,

I am your biggest fan.

Love you always!

My Husband

Thoughtful is your love,

Tender is your touch.

Hold me in your arms,

I love you so much!

Blow me a kiss,

To hold in my heart,

Even from a distance,

You are a part,

Of a life full of wonder,

Loving and care.

You are my true love,

And I want to be there.

Love you always!

Husband dear.

Special Son

My son I love you!

Time has made you a man.

Once cradled in my arms,

Now a man you stand.

Such a wholesome charm,

You display so well.

Tender and kind,

I know you'll do well!

You have a respect for life,

An eagerness to grow.

Inside and out,

I love you so!

May God shine on you,

In a full splendid way.

Bringing light and love to you,

Every single day!

My First Born Son

There once was a child,

He was born to me.

My first born son,

Who always sat on my knee.

Always so quiet,

Always so good,

Always caring and understood.

God has blessed him

For honors he earned.

A fine young man he grew up to be,

Now going off to college and university.

Please follow your heart,

And do your best.

Knowing that you can come home and rest.

You've made me proud,

I knew you would.

God bless you, Son and all the best!

Our Wonderful Son

We have a young man,

Our son he is called.

Hockey he plays, all winter long,

Goal after goal, he scores, it is true.

Saying, Mom, here this is for you!

We shiver at sight for the boards are near,

But he usually is quick, not to fear.

For ducking he does,

And missing they do,

And scoring a goal he shoots the puck too.

Proud you have made us,

With all that you do.

May God bless you dearly,

We love you so much.

A fine young man, love will touch.

Thank-you son, for letting us be,

Your loving Parents for all to see!

Much happiness always!

My Second Son

As time goes on I must admit,

My second son is quite a hit.

You prove to me, day by day,

You are growing in a special way.

Eager to help, considerate and kind,

Knowing that true love you will find.

For special qualities you do show,

Your intense love for life does grow.

Reflected in sports,

Whether hockey, soccer or basketball,

You do your best, and that's not all.

You excel at school, while working too.

You make me proud, Yes you do!

I love you son, handsome and dark,

I have watched God shine on you from the start.

Take care, good luck and,

Thank you and God bless you son from my heart.

My Loving Son

Love knows no limits,

From mother to son.

Even as time passes,

My son is the one,

That keeps my heart beating,

Year in and year out.

First just your mother

Then a special Grandmom.

You're a worker, a doer.

I love your style.

I pray God shines on you for a good long while.

I've seen you grow family wise,

Tender and playful making family ties.

Thank you son, a man you stand.

As we grow older please hold my hand.

May God continue to bless you too.

I hold in my heart a tender spot for you!

Love and best wishes, Mom.

Son's Embrace

I hold in my heart a special memory or two,

And yes, son, many are of you.

From birth to middle age,

Many fond impressions have been made.

While time has quickly passed,

And I hope it's not too late.

To tenderly tell of the pride that does swell,

Within my heart and my soul,

I can see you do well.

With family and hobbies,

Children, birdwatching and gardening,

Your tender heart is always loving.

I love you son like only a mother can.

Thank you son, I am your biggest fan!

Here's hoping for you,

May all your dreams come true!

Hugs and kisses love your mom.

Special Grandchild

Awesome is life,

For loving gifts are free.

Our son once a child,

Is a father soon to be.

With a smile on our face,

And love in our hearts,

We welcome your newborn,

And want to take part,

Of the joy and the laughter,

The cuddling and care.

Bringing us together,

With the love we share.

Congrats, New daughter and son.

You have blessed us through and through.

We pray God hands you happiness,

For little baby and both of you.

Love, hugs and kisses,

From Mom and Dad too!

Brotherly Love

Just last night a thought came to mind,

I suddenly realized

My brother is one of a kind.

When we were kids, in mischief we got.

Playing around, we sometimes fought.

You were always near, my shadow I thought.

Being close together, we were a lot.

As time went on and we grew up,

Separate life paths, we did adopt.

Physically apart, our love still remains,

Close, sincere, and supporting in life games.

The treasures we did find,

As our childhood did unfold,

Have proven to be many blessings untold.

You are my brother; I admire your style.

I pray our love goes that extra mile.

Heres hoping for you in abundance of love.

Trust in your heart,

And glance up – above,

Live life with a flare.

I am your sister and will always care.

My Special Brother

On this special day I'd just like to say,

I have memories made from yesterday.

My dear brother, You,

Whom in years gone by,

Was a minor pain in my side.

As we grew and we did mature,

While time fell in place.

I truly realized my love for you,

Was growing with God's grace.

I never knew you meant so much.

From my heart I want you to know,

Best wishes, Bro, please keep in touch!

With memories made, my heart is filled,

Gladness and love we did build!

May your tomorrow's shine

Sunny, Bright and Wonderful

Till the end of time.

My Caring Uncle

My Uncle, My Uncle.

So special you are!

Never a visit passes,

That you haven't made me your star.

All of my childhood,

On your knee I would sit,

Playfully wrestling,

Jostling a bit!

I remember each moment,

With tenderness in my heart.

And yes, Uncle,

You are a major part!

Of my most precious moments,

And I want you to know.

I pray God blesses you.

May you reap what you sow.

May love, care and good health,

Be yours to behold.

Thank you, Uncle

From the bottom of my heart!

Section Six:

A Congratulations Celebration

Precious Baby Boy

Congratulations!

I heard who is new.

You now have a baby boy,

All dressed in blue.

Hockey and cars are headed your way,

Plus many fun times day to day.

Sons are a blessing for mom and dear dad,

The joy that they bring make the family glad.

A precious son, so precious is he,

Love sent from heaven,

For all to see.

Congratulations again!

Congratulations

A bouquet of roses
A bouquet for you!
Here's hoping and praying,
All your life dreams come true!

Look through the window,
The window to your heart.
Eyes shining brightly
As you do start.

A career with a future,
Dawning new hopes.
Tending and caring,
As you learn the ropes.

May the thread of excitement,
Hold true for all time.
I pray God shines brightly
As success you do find.
Congratulations and best wishes
For your future.

Wedding Toast

A toast to the groom,

A toast to the bride.

Now you walk side by side.

Down the church isle,

Reaching far into life.

Holding and caring,

Dreaming dreams filled with spice.

Love and respect are yours to hold

Growing old together

We pray God does unfold.

Together each memory you make,

As a new man and wife.

We see in your eyes,

A bright sparkle of life.

Happiness, prosperity and love,

We wish for both of you

Congratulations!

And God bless you too!

Your New Home

Congratulations!

The news just arrived.

A new home for a couple,

Is new and splendid inside.

A new chapter of life,

To be shared by yourselves.

Making decisions and memories,

Sprinkled with love from above.

We are so happy,

To share in the fun.

We know you'll be thrilled,

As your new home is the one,

To go home to at night,

To play in by day.

We can't tell you enough,

How we feel this way.

May God enter in,

And bless those inside.

Making your home a blessing

And a blessing in for you to reside!

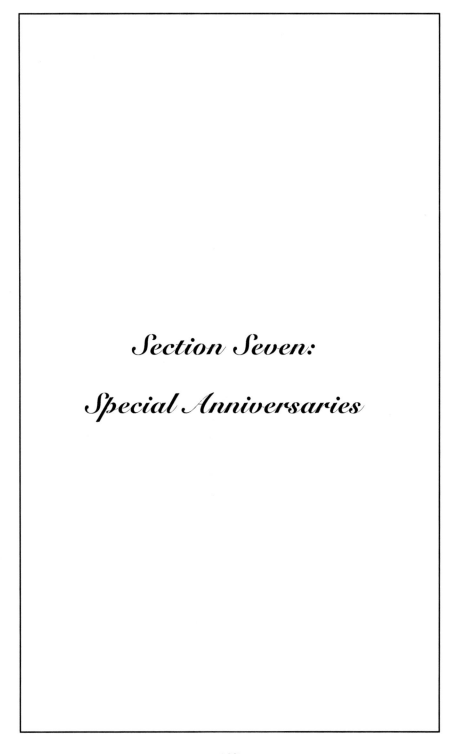

Section Seven:

Special Anniversaries

From The Bottom Of My Heart

All through the years,

You've been by my side.

Growing deeper in love,

Since you made me your bride.

Never did I know,

The true meaning of love.

As each day passes,

I know God is watching from above.

Your tender touch,

Whether my lips or my hand.

The bond only grows,

I barely understand.

I only know,

There has never been,

A more precious hour,

As the last ten years I've seen.

Hold me, kiss me, love me,

I pray we continue to soar,

Through life's adventures,

Ever after and more.

From the bottom of my heart,

I love you.

25ᵗʰ Anniversary

Your special moment has finally come

You've waited for years, one by one

The two of you have grown so close

Twenty-five years are yours to boast

Never forgetting the other one

Even though a time or two

A difference of opinion you had to bare

Yes, lovingly you did care

You pulled it off

You met each need

Caring and sharing you sowed the seed

Twenty-five years have come and gone

While your love has really shone

You've both been tried along life's way

Now we celebrate your special day!

///

Together Forty Years

The spirit of love,

Blows quietly on the wind.

Entering your hearts

As this anniversary wish sends.

My brother and wife,

Now joined hand in hand,

Heart to heart,

We see you strongly stand.

For forty years,

You have grown in care,

Love, joy and sweetness,

Are yours to share.

Congratulations, Brother and wife!

We love you deeply,

As you fulfill each others life

May your sweet love continue,

To grow day by day.

May God bless you both!

Sprinkled by the spirit of love's sunny day.

Hugs and Kisses to you both!

Happy Golden Wedding Anniversary

Today we gather to celebrate,

A voyage of love, struggles and faith.

From sea to sea, town to town,

Only God knew what would abound.

As time did pass, your family grew,

The tree of life became strong by you.

In your eyes were a vision,

Your hearts carried hope.

Blended with love you did more than cope.

Many trials were overcome,

While life abundantly came through,

Now we'd like to say, Mom and Dad

We love and are proud of you.

The priceless bands your fingers wear,

Have been blessed with honor, love and care.

Your nurturing spirits shines through like gold.

Happy 50th Anniversary with boundless love untold.

Graduation

Your stepping through a door,

A door from your past.

Entering the future,

It's your twelfth year at last.

Be proud, be glad,

Rest assured,

As your path unfolds,

Look life in the eye,

Reach, reach and try!

With faith and courage,

Reap the rewards.

Wonders and love,

Accomplishments and more.

May God guide you gently,

As you remember in awe.

The path that has lead you,

Through this Graduation door.

In Sincere Gratitude

For many caregivers,

In our mother's life.

The deeds that were completed,

Were more than nice.

Our mother, often spoke,

Of genuine care and love.

For she was the recipient,

Of the spirit from above.

If people were the flowers,

It is easily said.

Not just a rose bud,

But by a bouquet she was lead.

Through golden years, in the purest form.

Day by day, your care did adorn,

Her life, her love, her spirit too.

Your smiles, your touch,

May God Bless You.

May you find happiness at the end of your rainbows.

Section Eight:

Romantic Encounters

My Loving Sweetheart

Time has sewn a ribbon,

Through our hearts with care.

Never a moment passes,

That I forget we are a pair.

At a distance I first saw you,

Lovely, delicate and sweet.

Little did I know,

You would make my life complete.

Now you have gently laced,

My days full of love.

Silently I thank the Lord,

As he watches quietly from above.

Tenderly you touch me,

In more ways than you know.

Growing old beside you,

In a blessing hoping to unfold.

My Ladies Love

Gentle as a lamb,

Soft as a dove.

Hold me in your arms,

Let me share my love.

My heart has been filled

Like never before.

Your tender smile

Opens a new door.

Precious you are

My soul mate I've found

My love from the start

Grows deep and abounds.

Your perfect face

Your gentle touch

Your caring mind

I love and need so much.

Hold me, kiss me

Watch our love grow

I pray God shines brightly

As we do sow,

Precious memories now and throughout eternity.

Forever Love

Honey, I love you.

I'd like to take the time

To let you know again

I'm so happy your mine.

From the very beginning

You lit a special spark

You stood above the rest

Within my mind, soul and heart.

I hope I can give you,

All that you desire,

My love for you will never die.

Let me hold you tight again,

Let me smell the fragrance of your hair.

God has given me your hand

In marriage with delicate care

Whispering Love

Soft as a whisper

Gentle as a breeze

Warm as the sun

I love you with ease.

Tenderly you hold me

Gently you kiss

Never a moment passes,

I wouldn't miss

Your bright sunny smile

The twinkle in your eye

The calmness in your voice

As we happily reminisce

Thank you Sweetheart

For the coffee in the morning,

The flowers to my door

Your eager happy heart

I will cherish forever more

His Deepening Love

Look in his eyes

Look in his heart.

Gestures of love,

Begin to take part,

In a life full of wonder, trusting and care,

With kind words whispered in my ear.

Self-esteem building,

Calming each fear,

Knowing each thought,

Giving a loving stare.

I know you love me.

Words can't describe,

The faith that has grown,

In abundance, deep inside.

What you have given,

No person can steal.

I'll love you always.

You loving me, I do always feel.

To Dream A Dream

When once a girl was I,

Times were hard,

And I did try.

A dream I had,

Plus many more,

Came to my sleep,

True love was instore.

Some dreams came true,

While others were frizz.

I prayed to God,

To help me live.

Through trial and hurt,

I grew inside.

I say my thanks, now,

As we do thrive.

For God has given,

Pure love to hold

Thank you dear,

I say quite bold

You make me whole,

My partner, my best friend.

I pray our love will never end.

Hugs, and kisses now to Eternity.

Honey, I Love You

My love I give to you.

I want you to know.

To love is to surrender,

To love is to let go.

To love is to hear,

To love is to grow.

A whisper is a statement,

A smile is a gesture.

The twinkle in your eyes,

Makes my heart beat faster.

You are my sunshine,

Making life itself glow.

I carry your love,

Deep in my heart, you know

Thank you, honey.

May God shine on you,

All the days of your life.

Sweetheart, My love is for you.

Kitchen Reflection of Love

Stop, look and listen,

My sweetheart is in the kitchen.

Supper going strong,

As my sweetheart sings a song.

Every item blended,

Is a treat made with love.

Stirring and tasting,

Adding a few drops from above.

A sprinkle of this,

A sprinkle of that.

Oh, only if he knew,

His special touch of giving,

Makes my love for him shine through.

God Bless you, Special Partner.

My love for you is real.

I want you to know,

My heart you did steal.

Thank you, Love you forever!

Section Nine:

Friendships

Forever Friends

Friends are forever

True friends are few

Hopefully life gathers friends for you

Be it hello on a street while passing by

Or telephone call to just say hi

Lean on a friends shoulder

Or offer your sleeve

Give reassurance

But show them you won't leave

Caring and trusting

Are the makings of love

Given to all is from above

God loved us first

So let us show too

In abundance and warmth

The love that friends find coming from me and you

Precious Friend

You are my friend,

I've mentioned before.

You are a dear,

And I love you more.

As each day passes,

Our friendship grows,

With deep concerns,

A dependability soars.

We have a trust,

That we've learned to share.

Through our friendship,

We've learned to care.

When I am down,

You gently tell,

Hold on, take care,

I am your pal.

With all this said,

I want you to know.

Your friendship grows,

Deep within,

My heart and soul.

Thank you friend and God Bless!

Friends Always

Hello, Hello

Just dropping a note to say

You've been on my mind

On this very special day.

I remember when.....

We laughed and played,

Ate dinner, shopped,

Raised children along the way.

My memories are vivid,

Of your smile and laugh

Keep me in mind,

As you attend your daily tasks.

Remember our joy,

We found within,

Remember our love,

As sometimes we sang.

You are my friend,

Precious you are to me.

Our world has been

The best it could be.

May God shine on you.

Like you shone on me.

Working Friend and Pal

Pal, Side by side we worked,

Many goals we shared.

Growing through fun and toil,

Throughout many a year.

Now you are gone,

But with you I will be.

For faith in God gives us all life eternally.

You've enriched my life,

As we went through hard work and play.

Now I pray God shines on you,

In a very special way.

I know we will meet again,

Once more, up above.

Because the feelings that shine through

Are made with caring, brotherly love.

My Friend

The time has come,

To say goodbye.

Fun we have had,

And I know why.

You are my friend,

Through thick and thin.

The bond of love,

Spreads within.

As our friendship grows,

Years pass on by.

Growing older,

We do cry.

For parting hurts,

As only parting can.

Keep in touch,

For I care for you,

Very, very much!

Section Ten:

Camping Bliss

Campfire Pleasures

Listen to the quiet,

Not a sound to hear.

Nestled in the forest,

There with a baby dear.

People by their campfire,

Soaking up the peace.

Cup of coffee sipping,

While the dogs on a leash.

As I look all around,

Many pleasures to behold.

Some people walking by,

As the fire goes cold.

The sun lowers in the sky,

A day is nearly done.

Enjoy a good nights sleep

And wake up with the morning sun.

Campground Sounds

Sit by the table,

Look up at the tree.

Hear the Meadow Lark,

Singing merrily.

Many trailers parked

All along the grass

Big ones, Small ones

What a gas!

Playfully in the playground

Children running wild

Expending their energy

With a high pitched sound.

Now overhead, hear the flying geese.

Honking in a V form

Noisily, flying North east.

Camping Neighbor

Someone sitting in a lawn chair,

Someone new to me.

Makes a friendly gesture

And smiles happily.

Campings not for everyone

But new friends can be made.

Relax, sit down

Enjoy the summer shade.

Coffees on

Sandwiches too

Making friends while camping

Is easy to do.

Thanks for the visit

Your company was great!

I'll always remember

Our Super camping date!

Lakeside Birds

Down along the road,

Just around the bend,

Lies a piece of water,

Where the birds do tend.

Nurturing eggs and ducklings,

On the waters shore

Noisily protecting,

The eggs that they bore.

Many beaks, eyes and feathers

Adding to the clatter.

Soon they will also fly,

As they grow fatter.

This is the home,

Of geese, ducks, and the like.

Quiet only comes

Deep within the night.

Lake's Fun

Boats racing,

Pulling boys and girls.

Water splashing,

As fisherman cast their lures.

The lake is busy,

People everywhere.

Many laughing

As onlookers stare.

Birds flying

As clouds cast their shadow.

Keeping cool

Is the main matter.

Enjoy your self,

Relax a bit.

Catch a wave of water

See the beauty first hand

Or walk on the shore's sand.

With your favorite partner.

Fishermans Love

Peaceful and quiet

On the lakeside shore.

Scanning the hillsides,

While baiting our lures.

Gracefully flying,

Birds do soar.

Beneath white clouds,

We fish some more.

Silence, then wait

The rod does bend.

Excitement mounts

As the fisherman tends.

A fish, a fish,

What more can we ask for?

So Long

The weekends come and gone,

Now we must depart.

The trailers loaded up,

As we begin to start,

Our journey home is waiting.

Our farewells said and done.

Looking back we remember,

Our memories full of fun.

Goodbye, so long, farewell.

Hope to keep in touch,

As we drive down the road,

Following the westward sun.

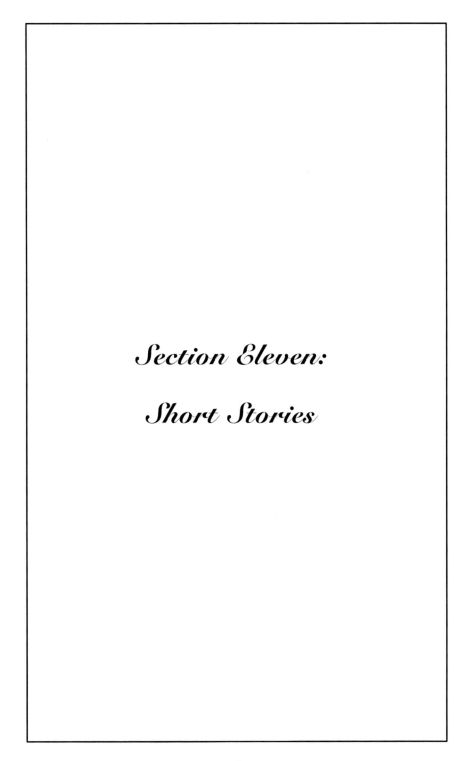

Section Eleven:

Short Stories

Calming Whispers

Skip along the path,
Beneath the sky of blue.
Angels whisper in your ear,
God is watching too!

Down comes the lovely rain,
Pitter, Patter it does go.
As it runs down the walk,
Green grass it does sow.

Now the rain has finally stopped
And birds do sing again.
Crystal clear is the air
While clouds are free from rain.

Rainbows are pretty,
Rainbows fill the sky.
Find the box of treasure
As we sing a soft lullaby.

Tuck your pillow in a ball,
Curl up good and tight.
Close your precious eyes,
And whisper a sweet good-night.

Butterfly, Butterfly

Butterfly, butterfly where have you been?
Among the bushes, in the air
On my shoulders, everywhere?

You are so pretty, spots and all
Fluttering softly, roses call
Now I see you, now I don't
Among the bushes, flies your soft coat.

Fly to the sun on a majestic day
Laughing with the children as they play
The puppies will chase you
Don't worry though, for God smiles in a sun-ray.

Butterfly, butterfly where have you been?
Looking so closely it has been seen
Around the world ever so gently
Kissing the flowers, bushes and trees
Never ending the butterfly sees.

Loving and kind, giving and sharing
Fly in the sunlight, for you are preparing
Bright summer days, into
Shining summer nights
Fall is coming, ending
Long summer thoughts.

Love transmitted through your glowing way
Thank you butterfly, for you are special today.

Birds of a feather

Soaring through the air
Birds of a feather
Swooping down without care
Only to endure all weather

Fly to the sun on a beautiful day
Circling the trees, in and out at play
Softly landing on grass green from rain
Only waiting to soar over and over again

One by one little chickees are born
Crack goes the shell, it is now torn
Out peeks a beak and little eyes too
Mommy bird is quick and knows what to do

Wait, what do I hear?
Yes, mother hears a worm for baby bird dear
Quietly walking on the velvety grass
Quick as a wink she has a worm for her catch

Chirp, chirp the baby birdies cry
Now momma bird brings the wonderful worms by
Soon not one will cry for worms or bread
"Soon I will fly", the little ones said

As each spring passes on by
The little birdies soon try
To be like mommy birdie
And leave their nest in the big old tree

Now they are grown
And have nicely flown
From treetop to fence
And onto bigger events!

Prairie Pride

Onward, onward,

Up and over,

Round and about,

Slowly climbing,

That old dirt road.

Mile after mile,

The sun does shine.

Blue sky, white clouds,

Bump, bump, bump,

Hole in the road.

Fields full of color.

Wheat swaying in the wind.

Journey onto an unknown road.

Saskatchewan,

Home of the prairie

Section Tweleve:

Special People Titles

Along Life's Path

My Special God Parents

A timely treasure,
Was given to me.
A God Mother and Father,
From birth you see.

On special occasions,
And birthday times too.
Memories were made,
That only God parents can do.

You loved and encouraged me,
Time, time and again.
My parents knew,
Your love would never end.

Special you are,
And loved you are too.
Thank you dearly,
May God shine on you!

A Secret Pal

Here is a little,

Something for you.

A token of care,

Wrapped in blue.

A secret Pal,

A secret friend,

A secret gift,

Meant just for you.

You do not know it,

But our thoughts are one.

I'm with you always,

In our secret hearts song.

Take care, Good luck,

Remember, God is good

He'll lead and guide you.

So you won't get lost

You're on my mind,

You're in my heart.

God bless you friend.

May the breath of goodness,

Breeze through your life.

My Teacher

When I first walked in uncertainty overcame me.

My guards were up and my muscles were stiff.

I found a desk and slowly sat down.

To my surprise your voice was tender.

You called my name and as I remember.

You showed warmth and caring as each lesson rendered.

You overcame any fear I had of an unfair teacher.

That would probably make me sad.

I learned to trust you.

I learned something each day.

You became my mentor and made my learning – play.

You taught me to soar, mentally and emotionally.

You gave me praise when my work was good.

Confidence building, as only a teacher could.

You pointed me along the most productive path.

And always helped me with my math.

Thank you teacher

For the support and gentle nurturing

You always have!

Section Thirteen:

Nature Sets The Scene

Beauty In Many Forms

Beauty as we know it
Stems from many things,
Colors radiant and alive,
Are true as the Blue Jay sings.

Beauty comes in many forms,
Perhaps you know a few.

A tender smile, perhaps a kiss,
Or just a sky of blue.

There is no limit what we behold,
For beauty is a form of love,
We see it in many things,
Precious gifts from above.

Stop and see all our precious gifts,
Give to other and know.

Lovingly from our lips,
As we see beauty grow.

Dream Catcher

See what tomorrow holds for you

Follow your dreams and know it is true

Take every opportunity and hold on tight

Given from above is the splendid light

The sparkle, the twinkle in your eye

Follow your dreams, it shall not die

The sky's the limit, please don't be timid

Take courage and dare to live life with flare

Enjoy the challenge one by one

Don't give up until their done

Reap the rewards, big and small

And remember always to walk tall

Growing and learning as each dream comes true

Ending each day you'll be much richer too!

Mountains Secrets

Majestic mountains stretching wide.

Strong, yet poetic, the trees are beside,

The calm, teal mirrored water,

Spreads for a mile.

The Loons swim and dive in graceful style.

The sun beats down on a radiant scene,

Where calm, pure stillness is sure to be seen.

Rocks outline the shallow shore,

And the wilderness is calling me to see and hear more

Of the Loons crying out loud,

In the still, breathless air.

Mountains on guard without a care.

Yes, this is beauty in the truest form.

Majestic and wholesome.

The wilderness has been born.

Babbling Brook

Down the trail,

Beside the road,

Behind the bushes,

Rushes the flowing brook.

Quiet air, mosquito free,

The only sound is the babbling brook,

Rushing on, around the bend.

Like life that never ends.

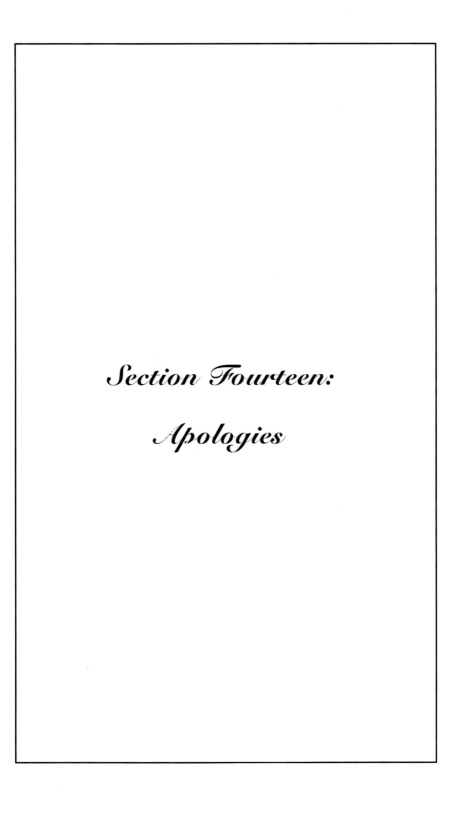

Section Fourteen:

Apologies

I'm Sorry

Yes, I know I've been a bore,

Now I come to you and ask for more.

More forgiveness, That is,

That only you can give

I was wrong, I will admit

I'm sorry and I do give

My apology and more.

Section Fifteen:

Faith To Stand By

I'll Be With You

Today I heard your pain,

I heard your plea for help.

Sorrow overcame me,

Because I want to help.

No one knows what tomorrow brings,

Except the Lord Himself.

Turn to God and ask for help.

As we are down and out.

Trials are overcome.

With faith we grasp His hand.

He will never let us down,

Even though we cannot stand.

I am your friend,

I can't do much

But beside you I will be.

My heart has a special spot.

Carved with love for thee.

If talking is what you need.

I will listen too.

God bless you friend.

I pray, your troubles are few!

Life

Day after Day
Life goes on
The sun comes up
The sun goes down

Babies are born
People die
Emotions rise
Emotions ebb

Life is ever enduring
And ever forgiving
Life is a miracle
From the beginning

Enjoy the laughter
Endure the pain
See the beauty
It's not just in your head

Know God is worthy
Know God is truth
Enjoy the beauty
And the gift of life

Know God is time
Never-ending
Ceaseless
And forgiving
Life is precious to the living

Growing Faith

Light your candle and carry it high
For the faith that God gives grows by and by
Through sorrow and hurt
Hurdles and stress
Give it to God, have faith and rest

God sees our pain and wants us to know
He will carry us through the deepest blow
True faith doesn't grow overnight you see
It's time after time that God rescues you and me

Each time the rescue seems to take place
A deeper faith in which truth does ride
Again God proves to be by our side
He lifts us up and carries us through
And changes our lives when we kneel and ask him to

Help us Lord with whatever we need
Bless us richly as we believe
Make our paths smooth, joyous and full of love
Giving to us faith, strong from above

And with it Lord, guide us down life's proper path
For on the straight and narrow we will last
Eternal life, God has promised to us
To all His children, where faith has grasped

Glory to God, awesome creator
Thank you Dear Lord, forever and ever Amen

Divine Love

Father, we thank Thee.

You reach us with Your Love.

You hear our silent groan,

And send your spiritual Dove.

Everytime we falter,

You never cease to care.

Holding us up firmly,

In times we cannot bare.

Even in the darkness,

Depression hits us bad,

But God's light falters not,

As Christ's light makes us glad.

Long for tomorrow.

See what God can do.

Pray to our Lord above,

He is preparing love and life for me and you.

Unending Promises

Softly the rain falls,

What can be in store?

Don't give up, but ask for more.

More love, more life, more adventure you see.

God will not leave you stranded, does he?

He promises life, delivering to you.

He has proven to all who have asked him to.

We have shown our faith and took off our masks.

The mask of sorrow, anger and hurt,

And suspicions that sometimes lurk.

God's word is holy, kind and never ending,

Rest assured His love is unending,

Reach out with faith,

Like a reflection in a mirror,

The answer will come crystal clear.

Know God will hold us in times of fear,

I pray our faith grows stronger year after year.

Reach For The Stars

Reach, Reach for the stars,

Live out your dreams,

Believe in your hearts.

Amazing things can come true,

When you kneel and ask our Lord to,

Answer prayers unsaid,

While knelt beside your bed.

Glory unseen,

Is our precious King.

Jehovah, Counselor, Holy one too,

Second to none for me and you.

Father our keeper,

Day and night,

Keeps us with His awesome might.

Love only knows the power He has.

As daily is seen through a looking glass.

Glow, rejoice, savour His love.

Radiate warmth given from above.

Thank you dear Savior

Your blessings are real,

Your Grace and forgiveness, I do feel.

He Cares

Yesterday, yesterday,

Lonely and sad,

Friends were few,

Love was bad.

Then into my life,

Came the precious Son.

Loving and caring,

Honoring each dream

And I now have contentment

From the Majestic King.

He heard my first plea.

He quickened to say,

I love you dear child,

For all the people to see.

Miracles did and do happen.

I'm sure not to just me.

God promises life, abundantly.

So grant me love and life,

Eternally Dear Lord.

And thank you my savior,

As I eagerly wait for more. Amen

Father's Grace

Blessed be the Lord,

Blessed be His love.

Rejoice in His grace,

Widespread from above.

Know He will hasten,

To heal the broken heart.

Walk in His light,

And be a part,

Of a life full of promise,

Adventure and more!

Thank you my Lord,

I do adore,

The life, the joy,

The contentment, the peace.

All You have in store!

Glory to our awesome God,

As I eagerly wait for more.

Thank you Father – Amen.

Dear Loved One

Soft as a whisper,

Is this time at hand.

Softly and quietly,

God holds your hand.

Be strong, be still

Turn fear away.

Gently call on God today.

See his angels stroke your hair.

As you lay and prepare,

To behold great things,

That lie ahead.

Friend, I'd like to say,

God is with you on this day

Our prayers are with you

And may God comfort you too,

Always and today!

Love on an Angel's Wing

As time has it, memories are made.

We often remember you as a child we played.

The first step you took,

The first word you said.

To the hour of graduation, at the head.

Your smile, your laugh,

Or perhaps a tear.

Precious child of ours,

Your memories are dear.

We don't understand why it had to end.

But we do believe God did send.

His promise of love, on an angels wing.

For someday coming we will sing.

Together we are, together we will be

For in our hearts you live eternally.

We thank God for the gift of time he gave.

You are our child and we do save.

Each precious memory that was made.

A tear, a kiss.

Eternally Mom and Dad

Winter's Frolic

Stop, Look, Listen

See the tree tops glisten.

Furry hat's, knitted scarves,

Fuzzy mittens, cold tree barks.

On the hill,

The snow has fallen.

Frolic, run, play and feel

Keeping warm.

As you do sail,

Down the coulee,

Down the run.

Enjoy the cool,

Enjoy the sun.

Winter games,

For young and old.

The snow has come,

And now it's cold.

Happy Winter to You and Yours!

Christmas In The Land

It's time, It's time,
To sing songs again.

Christmas has come,
In a splendid way.

Stars in the sky,
Making pictures above.
Angels looking down,
Whispering words of love.

The ground bright with snow,
Making our paths glow,
Giving us beauty,
As we go.

Snow falling softly,
Landing in the valley.

A pure white blanket lies,
Where the wild wolf cries.

Christmas carollers coming and going,
Wearing toques and scarves.

Singing songs of glory,
As they tell the Bethlehem story.

Yes, singing is good.

Singing is grand.

Sing your precious heart out,
Wide, throughout the land.

Here's hoping a Merry Christmas
To you and yours!

Christmas Treasure

The bond we've made,

As years have passed,

Has grown in strength,

I believe will last.

For through the thick,

As trouble does stew,

We cannot forget,

Our love for you!

Christmas has come,

With a light that shines,

Through trouble and hurt,

As we remember the good times.

Precious are friends,

Precious are you!

Love only knows what

Jesus can do!

Lift up your heart,

Rekindle the flame.

Look for the positive,

That is why God came.

Seasons Greetings and love to you both.

Soft Petal Poems

A Special "hello" to all who read
my poems. I hope my book is encouraging,
inspirational and a joy to share with others!

My hopes for each one of you are:
follow your heart, be true to yourself,
dare to live your dreams and know in
your mind that all things are possible
for those who believe!

God Bless
Lana C. Kuystermans

Printed in the United States
91360LV00007B/166-186/A